COLORFUL BLESSINGS COLORING BOOK

CRYSTAL
COLORING BOOKS

Copyright © 2018 Crystal Coloring Books
All rights reserved.

ISBN-13: 978-1986527682
ISBN-10: 1986527689

Count
Your Blessings
And
Smile
Everyday

God's
Blessings Are
Far Beyond
Anything You
Could
Dream Of

Each
Day
You Have
Is
A
Blessing

Friends
Are
A
Blessing

Be A
Blessing
Be A
Friend

May
You Feel
Blessed
Today And
Always

God
Gave Me Such
A Blessing
When
He Gave Me
You

It's
A
Blessing
To Have Someone
Like
You

Our
Greatest
Blessing
Is Being Loved
And Loving
Others

Enjoy
Blessings
All
Year Long

Thank
You
Lord
For
Blessing
Me

God
Really Did
Something
Special When He
Blessed Me With
You

Thak You
For
Blessing Me
with
A wonderul
Life

Your
Love Is
My
Greatest
Blessing

May
Your Troubles
Be Less
And
Your Blessings
Be More

When I Started Counting My Blessings My Life Got So Much Better

This
House Is
Blessed
With Love
And
Happiness

May
Your Day
Be
Blessed
With
Happiness

May
The Lord
Bless
Us With
Happiness
Love And
Faith

May You
Be Blessed
Abundantly Today
Tomorrow
And The Rest Of
Your Lives

COLOR TEST PAGE